Finding God Through

Acronyms

(and other fun stuff)

Finding God Through

Acronyms

(and other fun stuff)

Volume 3

By
Farley Dunn

THIS IS A MYCHURCHNOTES.NET BOOK

PUBLISHED BY MYCHURCHNOTES.NET

COPYRIGHT © 2016 BY FARLEY DUNN

www.mychurchnotes.net

Finding God Through Acronyms (and other fun stuff)/Farley Dunn – 1st ed.

Vol. 3

This is an original work created by Farley Dunn for the website MyChurchNotes.net.

All rights reserved.

ISBN: 978-1-943189-20-5

www.ThreeSkilletPublishing.com

Non-public domain scripture quotations are from The Holy Bible, English Standard Version® (ESV®), copyright © 2001 by Crossway, a publishing ministry of Good News Publishers. Used by permission. All rights reserved.

Dedication

To Terry Godwin.

Dessert always came first. What an excellent way to live!

MyChurchNotes.net

Table of Contents

Our AIRY God	15
Our ANORAK God	21
Our BACKPACKING God	25
Our BEACH God	29
Our BRIGHT God	33
Our CIDER God	37
Our CRISP God	43
Our FAN God	45
Our FLEECE God	49
Our FRISBEE God	53
Our GARDEN God	57
Our HARVEST God	63
Our HOODIE God	67
Our JULY God	71
Our LUSH God	75
Our NIPPY God	79
Our PICNIC God	83
Our RECREATION God	87
Our RIPE God	91
Our SEA God	93
Our SPICE God	97
Our TENDER God	103
Our TRIP God	107
Our VIBRANT God	111
Our WINDY God	117
Our YAM God	121
Coming to Christ in Three Easy Steps	125

Introduction

God has a sense of humor.

He wants us to go *Backpacking* with him, throw a *Frisbee*, and wrap up in our *Hoodie* when the weather grows cold. He takes us on a *Trip*, protects us when it's *Windy*, and feeds us *Yams* when we grow hungry.

It seems God's thought of everything.

Finding God through Acronyms is a fun way to share Jesus and the Word of God with your children, friends, and coworkers. It's a good way to show them how much fun God wants us to have each and every day.

Enjoy God's Word as you've never seen it before.

Farley Dunn

Our AIRY God

*In **Worship** of Our Holy God*

Whether in a small plane, attached to a hang glider, or windsurfing off the Carolina coast, to catch air gives a feeling of exhilaration that cannot be matched by sitting in front of a television. We need the wind in our face, the breeze whipping our hair, and the intake of fresh, outside air in our lungs.

In short, we need to partake of life in a new and visceral way. That's what God does for us. He makes life new, makes life real, and makes life visceral. He is the air we breathe, and the excitement that comes with each day. He is our buoyant, vivacious, and AIRY God.

Let's take a look at our AIRY God:

A – He gives himself to ALL those who come to him for new life.

Acts 2:17 tells us that in the last days (which are now) God will pour out his spirit on ALL those who wish to come to him.

The Scriptures don't provide an exclusion to this promise. It's not just for the Baptists or Episcopalians. It doesn't exclude Muslims or agnostics. Anyone who comes to him in belief and trust will receive a full measure of the Lord's infilling and power; and it will be a breath of fresh spiritual life, lifting us on high.

I – He is our INTERCESSION, a buffer between our humanity and our spiritual inheritance.

Romans 8:26 teaches how God, through the Holy Spirit, makes INTERCESSION for us. In those times when we feel weighted down with our problems, we can be lifted up into the glories of the Father, in whose presence we will be filled with God's joy.

R – His name is REMEMBERED in all generations.

Psalm 45:17 tells of David's upwelling of praise for the Lord, but what he says is still true today. Our great and glorious Lord is here yesterday, today, and forever. He will never leave us or forsake us. We can come to him when we are down, and he will lift us up.

Y – He is the beginning and end of all things, our YEA and amen.

To call out YEA indicates excitement. It's also a word of introduction to an important statement. God is both. In 2 Corinthians 1:20 he is our YEA, our enthusiasm before the trials of this life, and he is the preface to the most important things we say. He adds power to our walk with him; in him we will never know defeat.

Our AIRY God gives bounce and life to our steps. When we walk in time with him, we will know the freshness of new life with every breath we take.

In summary, there is no better pick-me-up than to spend our day with God.

BIBLICAL
Trivia

You Didn't Know Was in the Bible

Genetic Engineering is a Biblical fact!

(Check it out in Genesis 30:37-39)

Our ANORAK God

*Finding **Faith** in the Word of Christ*

In the coldest depths of winter, there is only one garment that offers total protection. It is the ANORAK. More than a coat, and different than a parka, an ANORAK was invented by the Caribou Inuit for use in one of the coldest places on earth: the Arctic.

What makes it special? Its five major features: no front opening; a waterproof outer layer; a drawstring hood; drawstring cuffs; and a drawstring waist. This is a pull-over jacket designed to protect the wearer in the most extreme weather.

That's what our God does for us. He protects us in the most extreme situations we might encounter.

Let's look at our ANORAK God:

A – When the world is against us, God is our AVENGER.

2 Samuel 18:31 tells of a life-changing moment in the story of king David. The Cushite comes to him after the battle, and he informs the king, "This day the Lord has AVENGED you of all who rose against you."

N – He gives us NOURISHMENT so that we may have strength in our need.

Genesis 50:21 reveals Joseph as an archetype of Christ. He tells his brothers to not be afraid, because he will NOURISH them, and they will want for nothing.

O – Christ loves each ONE of his children as much as he loves himself.

Luke 15:4 pulls back the layers of Christendom to show the heart of Jesus. If just ONE lamb is lost, he will do whatever it takes to bring that lamb back home.

R – He REMEMBERS us even when we think we are forgotten.

Genesis 9:15 reflects God's remorse after the Flood. He tells Moses he will REMEMBER his promises, and he will never again destroy all he has created. When God makes promises to us, he doesn't forget them, even when we don't see the results.

A – We are ALSO adorned with the breastplate of righteousness.

Leviticus 8:8 explains one of the layers of protection the Lord gives us. Our security is magnified, because in addition to our holy robes, he ALSO adorns us with a breastplate, not of iron, but of righteousness to protect us from all evil.

K – He KEEPS us in the palm of his hand, against the terror of the storm.

Numbers 6:24 quotes the blessing of Aaron over the children of Israel. "The Lord bless you and KEEP you." We are safely carried through whatever may come our way.

In summary, our best protection against the storms of life is the strong arms of our magnificent God.

Our BACKPACKING God

In Pursuit of the **Kingdom of God**

The majesty of the world is not seen from our living room easy chairs. Sometimes we have to explore God's creation to experience all he has made by his glorious hand.

And we're not talking about museums and shopping malls.

All the hills and sunsets and oceans are God's, and they are his gifts to us. When we go BACKPACKING with him, we will experience his wonders in a new and personal way.

Let's take a look at the majesty of our BACKPACKING God:

B – He brings the BRIGHTNESS of each morning to show his power over all the earth.

Psalm 18:12 says that out of the BRIGHTNESS of the Lord, the storms roll across the land, bringing hailstones and bolts of lightning.

A – He APPOINTS celebrations according to the movements of the heavens in honor of his greatness.

Psalm 81:3 tells us that at the time of the New Moon, we are APPOINTED to celebrate him with a festival of praise unto his name.

C – His CEDARS upon the hills are watered by his own hand.

Psalm 104:16 describes the great forests God has planted across the globe. It is by one of his hands that the CEDARS have been planted, and he cares for them with his other.

K – He calls upon the KINGDOMS of the earth to sing his praises.

Psalm 68:32 sends up the cry that every good thing in every KINGDOM comes from his hand, and all praises belong to him.

P – His PASTURES are his abundant supply and verdant gift.

Psalm 23:2 reassures us with that familiar verse: He maketh me to lie down in green pastures; he leadeth me beside the still waters.

A – He ANOINTS us with the very things he has created.

Psalm 23:5 assures us his worldly gifts are his blessings unto us, for he ANOINTS our heads with oil, even until all of our blessings can no longer be contained.

C – He CROWNS his children with his special blessings.

Psalm 8:5 shows us that all races are beautiful unto God, for he has CROWNED mankind with glory and honor.

K – The KNOWLEDGE of the Lord is as unfathomable as the farthest oceans that cover our world.

Psalm 77:19 speaks of the vastness of the seas and how we cannot comprehend the enormity of their depths.

I – His INHERITANCE to us is the land as far as we can see.

Psalm 105:11 reveals the breadth of his gifts to

us, for all of Canaan is ours, even as the land stretches to the distant horizon, and our minds cannot comprehend its end.

N – His NAME reminds us of all his wondrous works.

Psalm 105:1-5 tells us to remember his wondrous works by singing praises unto his NAME.

G – His GRASSES in the field show the depth of his love for us.

Psalm 72:16 incites a blessing upon Solomon, that his bounty from God will be as plentiful as the GRASSES in the field.

When we travel side-by-side with God is when we truly experience the wonders of his majesty and creation. Let's get out of our easy chairs and get on the road with him.

In summary, we experience what we touch, and God gives us his entire creation, if we just reach out for it.

Our BEACH God

*Finding **Faith** in the Word of Christ*

The heat of summer draws us to the ocean just as the pressures of life draw us unto God. In the same way that we are refreshed at the BEACH, so are we refreshed when we spend time with God.

Let's look at our BEACH God:

B – He is BEAUTIFUL to behold.

> David is the master psalmist. In Psalms 48:1-2, he sings a song of God, telling us that great is the Lord, and greatly to be praised. He is BEAUTIFUL, the joy of the whole earth.

> God is the sparkling sand in the morning light. He is the wave that crashes on the shore; the tide that renews the seas with life. He is the joy of the whole earth.

E – He ESTABLISHES his kingdom forever.

In Psalm 48:8, David tells us that the city of the Lord of hosts is magnificent, that God ESTABLISHES it unto the ends of the earth.

Visit the beach, and the sand seems to stretch into the distance. Return a decade later, and it's the same. In a hundred years, it will not change. That's the kingdom of God, always the same, never changing, waiting on us to return.

A – He ANOINTS us as his cherished children.

Psalm 23:5 tells us that God ANOINTS us, singling us out as his special creation. His love is a rising tide, sweeping around us, cleansing us of all life's impurities, and flowing from our cup to the world.

The beach – where sand meets sea – is God's sacred place, for only that which is covered by the hand of God can stand against the rising waters. When he holds his hand over us, the storms may rage. Yet, when the sun rises, the waves will eventually recede. After the storm passes, we will still stand at his side.

C – He CHOOSES to give us his very best.

In Psalms 47:1-4, David instructs the chief musicians to clap their hands, for it is God who

CHOOSES our inheritance. He will give gifts unto us according to the great gifts he once bestowed on Jacob.

God will smooth the way before our feet, as the waves smooth the sands on the shore. If we need material blessings, he will lay them before us. If it is spiritual strength we lack, it is his to offer. Nothing is too hard for God.

H – He is our HIDING PLACE.

When the storms of life battered David, he turned to the Word of God. In Psalm 119:114, he tells us the Lord is his HIDING PLACE and his shield.

When our world turns dark, and we can't find our way, God is the light thrusting upward in the storm. He is the beacon on the shore, and when we hide in him, the storm will not defeat us. We will look behind us and see only one set of footprints in the sand, and we will know that in the time of storm, he held us in his arms.

To summarize the message, when we spend time with God, he will renew and protect us, for he treasures his children.

Our BRIGHT God

*In **Worship** of Our Holy God*

The lengthening days of spring are a sure sign that summer is on the way. Kids crowd the streets on their bicycles, boats come out of garages, and hedges are clipped to a tee.

Our brains crave sunlight. Without it, we sink into a melancholy state, and we are good for no one.

However, whatever the season, we have a BRIGHT light that shines upon us at all times. His name is Jesus Christ, the Son of God.

Let's look at our BRIGHT God:

B – He shines forth with the BRIGHT light of hope.

> In John's vision in Revelation 22, John is shown the magnificence of heaven, from the throne of God to the tree of life. In Verse 16, Jesus stands before him and proclaims, "I am the Root and

Offspring of David, the BRIGHT and Morning Star."

In that day there shall be no night, for the Lord God himself shall be the light that shines forever and ever.

R – His RAIMENT shines with holy radiance.

Jesus took Peter, John, and James to the mountain to pray. We read in Luke 9:29 that as he prayed, his appearance altered, and his RAIMENT glistened with heavenly light.

In the presence of his Father, even Jesus' lowly, homespun clothing became something of beauty.

I – He transforms us into his IMAGE.

In 2 Corinthians 3:14-18, we learn that we have been as blind men. However, as in a shining mirror, we see our IMAGE becoming more and more like that of Christ each and every day.

It is the brilliance of his holiness that others see in us.

G – His GLORY reveals his godhood to us.

The people gathered before the tabernacle of

meeting, and in Leviticus 9:6, Moses tells them that when they obey the commandment of the Lord, his GLORY will shine forth over them.

God treasures obedience more than sacrifice, and when we let him lead us, he shows us he is pleased with our actions.

H – His HANDIWORK shines down from the stars in the sky.

In Psalm 19:1, David tells us how the glory of God is found in the heavens, for the stars above are an example of his HANDIWORK.

When we doubt the incredible majesty of God, just step outside at night, and his awesome power shines down on us from a hundred billion points of light.

T – God lights his TABERNACLE with the fire of his presence.

After leaving Egypt, the children of Israel came to the edge of the desert. Exodus 13:21 describes how the Lord went ahead of the people, lighting the TABERNACLE as a pillar of fire in the night.

When our darkest day comes upon us, God is

the everlasting light that shows us where to place our next footstep.

To summarize the message, there is no darkness when we walk with God, for he shines with the light of his eternal glory.

Our CIDER God

*In **Worship** of Our Holy God*

Cider is a word that has different meanings in different parts of the world. In Europe and parts of South America, it's an intoxicating drink derived from fermented fruit. In North America it's normally considered a pleasant, non-alcoholic beverage.

No matter the part of the world we hail from, CIDER comes from the fruit of God's blessings upon the land. In truth, there is none sweeter than our CIDER God.

Let's look at our CIDER God:

C – He brings forth CLUSTERS of blessings.

> In Genesis 40:10, Joseph is interpreting the butler's dream. Little does Joseph know that his prediction of CLUSTERS of blessings for the butler is no more than a stepping stone for the

blessings that God will soon shower upon Joseph.

I – He is the IMAGE of the invisible God.

Colossians 1:15 tells us that God is the firstborn of every creature; the first fruit of the vine; and the creator of every good thing. When we see new life spring forth around us, we can know we see the IMAGE of the invisible God in our midst.

D – He is the DEW that brings forth the good fruit.

Zechariah 8:12 describes God as the DEW from the heavens that makes the seed prosperous and the vine to give her fruit. When God comes into our life, his presence brings blessings of increase.

E – He commands the EARTH to do his bidding.

Psalm 50:1 speaks to the mighty power of God, for the EARTH bends to his bidding, from the rising of the sun, to the going down of the same. When God speaks, the bounty of the EARTH rises forth, and he makes it ours.

R – He is the REWARDER of those that diligently seek him.

Hebrews 11:6 tells us the one thing we must have to please the Lord: Faith. If we come to him, we must believe he is the God of all creation, and in that moment, he will open his heavens unto us.

To summarize the message, all good things on the earth are God's, and when we believe in him, he will shower his goodness upon us.

BIBLICAL

You Didn't Know Was in the Bible

King Belshazzar owned the world's first iPad.

He received an email from God on it.

(Check it out in Daniel 5:5)

Our CRISP God

*Finding **Faith** in the Word of Christ*

When the north wind shifts the day from steamy to CRISP, we relish the change in the air. We draw in a breath, and the world feels fresh and new.

God is just like that. When our days begin to suffocate us, we can trust in the Lord to sweep over us, changing our circumstances until they are fresh and new.

Let's look at our CRISP God:

C – He CLEANSES us from the evil of this world.

> 1 John 1:7 tells of Christ's blood and how it CLEANSES us from all sin. In him we are made fresh and new.

R – He RESTORES us to our original condition.

> Psalm 23:3 reveals how he RESTORES our souls,

bringing us back to a renewed condition.

I – His IMMORTAL hand supports us forever.

> 1 Timothy 1:17 exposes the true nature of God, who is eternal, IMMORTAL, invisible, and the only wise God.

S – He SANCTIFIES his creation unto the day when he will return.

> 1 Thessalonians 5:23 assures us he SANCTIFIES us wholly, for we are made fresh and new in him.

P – He PERMITS all good things in our lives.

> Hebrews 6:3 underscores the totality of who God is, for he is the only one who PERMITS us to do all that we do.

When the winds of life seem to weigh us down, we can look forward to God's new day coming. He will caress us with freshness, and his CRISP revitalization will invigorate us once again.

To summarize the message, God sees our circumstances, and he knows just when we need a change.

Our FAN God

*Seeking **Hope** in Our Risen Savior*

August is the cruelest of the summer months. The heat has built during June and July, the fields have dried, and there seems to be no relief from the dog days that have replaced the glory of early spring.

How can we survive yet another night of sweltering heat beneath the moon of an August heat wave?

That's when we need to break out the FAN, for our bodies are naturally attuned to the cooling effects of a breeze during summer's worst times. The very perspiration that tells us the heat is up is what cools us when we step into the FAN'S refreshing breeze.

God is that FAN, coming to us in our most desperate times, and refreshing us with his cooling winds.

Let's look at our FAN God:

F – He grants us FAVOR in our daily walk through this life.

Job 10:12 tells of the FAVOR of God, for in Job's lowest time, he recognized that all goodness and life comes through the gracious hand of the Father.

A – He ANSWERS our cries of desperation so that we can know his relief.

Psalm 91:15 reassures us that the Father in heaven will ANSWER when we call unto him; he will be with us in our trouble; and he will rescue us and hold us in honor before the world.

N – He is the NEW commandment that lifts us to NEW heights in love.

John 13:34 speaks to Jesus' true purpose in life. He is the NEW way of thinking, the refreshment in the time of trial, the love that draws the world to the Father. He wants his NEW commandment to be first in our lives, that we truly love one another as he loves us.

It is the love of Christ that truly brings cooling relief in the heat of summer. When we let that love shine in us, it will be as a cooling FAN, and we will know the relief that God can provide.

In summary, when we show love to one another, all our other problems will seem to melt into the background.

Our FLEECE God

*Finding **Faith** in the Word of Christ*

Fabrics have certain properties, just as minerals are brittle or flammable, or plastics can be transparent or opaque. Some fabrics are designed to wick moisture from the skin, while others are windproof, fighting the debilitating effects of air against the skin in the coldest of weather.

Some of the most important properties of fabrics are temperature regulation. Lightweight fabrics allow body heat to escape. Heavier fabrics hold the heat better.

The best fabric for heat retention is fleece. Originally from sheered sheep, modern, lighter weight, manmade fleece is now made from synthetic fibers.

What is so great about fleece? It's rift with small air pockets that trap body heat, holding the warmth tightly against the skin, preventing the cold from burning our flesh.

That's our God. He's a FLEECE God, offering us protection against the bitter realities of a sinful world.

Let's look at our FLEECE God:

F – He FULFILLED the ancient prophecies that all might be washed clean.

Mark 15:28 reveals the extent of Jesus' love for us, for he let himself be numbered with the vilest sinners that we might be cleansed of our sins.

He FULFILLED the need for a sacrifice for our sins.

L – He is LORD of all creation, subject to no man's whim.

Colossians 1:15 speaks of Christ as the image of God. If we have seen one, we have seen the other. He is also the firstborn of all creation, and there is nothing he cannot command.

He is LORD over the evil of this world, and we can find our protection in him.

E – He is the EARTHQUAKE that releases the prisoner from sin.

Acts 16:26 relates the pivotal moment in the story of Paul and Silas. They were trapped in man's prison, and God's fist shook the earth, releasing them from their confinement.

Even the EARTHQUAKE from the bowels of the earth is at the command of our eternal God.

E – He ENDURES when all other protection falls away.

Psalm 19:9 encourages us with the eternal nature of our God, for we read that he is pure, his decrees are firm and righteous, and he ENDURES forever.

There is nothing under the heavens that can break loose God's protecting hand.

C – He is the CURE to our captivity in sin.

Jeremiah 33:6 speaks to a Judah and Jerusalem embroiled in battle with Babylon. Even as the children of Israel are on the brink of destruction, God proclaims his intentions to CURE the nation with peace and truth.

Israel had no power to save herself. The CURE had to come from God alone.

E – His covenant with mankind is EVERLASTING, never reaching an end.

Genesis 9:16 bares the true heart of God. In disgust at the wickedness of man, he brought a great flood upon the earth. Yet, when Noah praised God, God made an EVERLASTING covenant with man, leaving the rainbow as evidence of his vow to never again destroy the earth by flood.

Our praise draws God unto us, and the more we praise him, the tighter he draws.

In summary, it's when we keep our God tightly wrapped around us that he can insulate us from the devastating effects of a sinful world.

Our FRISBEE God

*Offering **Evangelism** to the World*

A plastic FRISBEE is an amazing toy. It's no more than a simple disk, but in the right hands, it can perform incredible feats of prowess.

God is the master of the FRISBEE, as he is the master of us. When we allow him to do with us as he wills, we will become champions for him.

Let's look at our FRISBEE God:

F – We are FEARLESS when our God is at our side.

> David was one of the greatest men in the Bible. Yet, when Saul pursued him, he was afraid, and he ran away and hid in a cave.
>
> Then, in Psalm 27:1, David cried out, "Whom shall I fear? The Lord is the strength of my life; of whom shall I be afraid?"

The difference was God. In him we are FEARLESS.

R – We are RENEWED by the infilling of the Holy Spirit.

Paul founded the church at Corinth, yet antagonists in Corinth rejected his authority, continually attacking him and his ministry.

It is in this context that we read 2 Corinthians 4:16. Paul wrote, "Though our outward man perish, yet the inward man is RENEWED day by day."

God's Spirit was Paul's stalwart inner strength, even though he was battered by the world.

I – We are redeemed in the IMAGE of the Father.

Adam was created in the IMAGE of God, and then he fell from grace. We read in Colossians 3:10 that when we put on the new man, we are renewed in the IMAGE of the one that created us.

It is the spiritual man that becomes like God, for Jesus came to redeem not the flesh, but the spirit.

S – We SPEAK with the tongues of angels.

> Jesus was crucified, and he rose again. For forty days he resided with the disciples, promising them another would come, bringing them power.
>
> On the day of Pentecost, they were gathered in the upper room. Acts 2:4 tells us that they were all filled with the Holy Spirit and began to SPEAK with other tongues.
>
> God gives us a companion that dwells in us, filling us with power every day.

B – We BURN within at the approach of the fearsome power of God.

> After arising from the tomb, Jesus appeared to Peter and Cleopas en route to a village called Emmaus. They did not know him. However, in Luke 24:32, their eyes were opened, and they turned to one another, saying, "Did our hearts not BURN within us, while he talked with us?"
>
> Even if we do not recognize the visible presence of God, our hearts will acknowledge his majesty and awesome power.

E – We EMBRACE the God that gives us life.

> In Solomon 8:1-3, Solomon speaks of us as his brothers, and in his pleading, he desires us to come into his mother's house, for he desires to EMBRACE us.

> His love is that of Jesus, who draws us unto him. When we EMBRACE Jesus, we enter into his throne room to abide with him forevermore.

E – We ENRICH the world around us.

> Psalm 65:9 tells us that the Lord visits the earth, and he enriches it with the river of God.

> We are made like unto God, and when we come to Jesus, we are reborn in his image. As emissaries of our heavenly Father, it is our job to ENRICH the fallow fields of this world.

To summarize the message, God sends us into the world to be his hand unto the people we meet. When we trust him, he will make us champions, enabling us to do things we never thought possible.

Our GARDEN God

*Offering **Evangelism** to the World*

When the world warms, and the soil is ready to offer sustenance to the seeds snuggled in its embrace, it's time to get our tiller in top shape. The ground needs turned and our shoulder put to the plow.

It's time to grow a GARDEN, to see new life burst forth, and to see the beginnings of the harvest right before our eyes.

Our walk with Christ is the same. The world is ready, we are the workers, and the seeds of God's Word are ready to plant. All the earth is God's GARDEN, and soon we will see the beginnings of his harvest waving in the breeze.

Let's look at our GARDEN God:

G – He GIVES his garden sustenance and energy

that it might produce a good harvest.

> 1 Samuel 2:10 tells us the Lord GIVES strength to his king, that his adversaries might be broken to pieces.

A – He ARRAYS his garden in beauty and splendor.

> Luke 12:27 says that the lilies that grow in the field are ARRAYED with more beauty than even Solomon in all his glory.

R – He takes the RUINS of winter's fallow fields and prepares them for the planting.

> Acts 15:16 relates the words of the prophet, for God will rebuild the RUINS of the tabernacle of David, which is fallen down.

D – He pulls up and DESTROYS all the weeds that sprout in our garden.

> 2 Chronicles 25:16 is our banner of joy, for this passage gives us the assurance that God will DESTROY the wicked who do not hearken to his counsel.

E – He is the sun and the rain, the ENDURING promise of a bountiful garden.

> Psalm 19:9 states his majesty, that the glories of

God ENDURE forever; his judgments are true and righteous.

N – His very NATURE is that of a seed, ready to sprout forth in new life.

Hebrews 2:16 helps us see God as he really is, for he refused the nature of angels; rather he took on him the seed of Abraham, becoming human that he might know our humanity.

This world is filled with a humanity that does not truly know him, and when we place the seed of Christ's message in the ground God has prepared, our harvest will be bountiful.

In summary, God wishes everyone to come to him, becoming part of the harvest, and he gives us the tools to plant his seed.

BIBLICAL *Trivia*

You Didn't Know Was in the Bible

Bald people rule!

They're also bad for your health!

(Check it out in 2 Kings 2:23-24)

Our HARVEST God

In Pursuit of the **Kingdom of God**

Working hard for a good reward is at the core of the American Dream. Whether it's that retirement home in the mountains or time to spend with our grandchildren, we expect our labors to pay off in the end.

Our Christian walk is the same. We want rewards, both spiritual and material, to come from our hard work for the Father.

Our God is the God of the HARVEST. He wishes to give us a good reward, and when we walk in his ways, he will send an abundance of blessings our way.

Let's look at our HARVEST God:

H – He is the joy in the HARVEST.

Isaiah 9 speaks of the coming of the Christ, and

in Verse 3 we see that the joy of the Lord comes as the joy in the ample HARVEST.

A – He meets all our needs with ABUNDANCE.

Job 36 tells of God's majesty and power. In Verse 31 we read not only of God's power to judge the earth, but also his generosity in providing his people sustenance in great ABUNDANCE.

R – He gives us generous RECOMPENSE for our faith in him.

Hebrews 10 teaches us of the glorious nature of our God. Verse 35 encourages us to keep our confidence in the Lord, for our RECOMPENSE for our faith will be great.

V – He clothes his people in the finest of VESTURES.

In Genesis 41:42, Pharaoh rewarded Joseph's interpretation of his dream by clothing him in VESTURES of the best fabrics in Egypt. Pharaoh was the manifest hand of God in Joseph's life.

E – He gives us flight on EAGLE'S wings.

Psalm 103:5 lifts us up with God's promises. Not only will we eat at a table of plenty, but our youth will be restored as the EAGLES that soar in flight.

S – He is STEADFAST before us, unto the end of all time.

Daniel 6:26 relates the power of the God of Daniel, for he is not only the living God, he is STEADFAST forever, and his kingdom will never be destroyed.

T – He sets us on the THRONE of heaven so that we might do great things for him.

In 1 Kings 2:24 king Solomon gives all credit to God, the one who established him and set him on the THRONE of David his father.

To summarize the message, God's rewards are so great that our earthly dreams pale in comparison.

Our HOODIE God

*In **Worship** of Our Holy God*

The coldest 30 days of winter tend to cross over from the end of January into the first of February. February 1st falls right in the middle, making it statistically the most frigid day in the entire year.

Burrr! It's time to dress warmly, from leggings for our ankles, and caps for our ears, to gloves to warm our hands.

Something that helps more than anything else is having a HOODIE next to our skin. It holds our body heat in, and keeps the air from seeping around our face.

God is like that. When we keep him close, he holds our spiritual heat in, and he keeps the sin of the world from getting to us.

Let's look at our HOODIE God:

H – He is our HELPER when the winter winds blow.

Hebrews 13:6 reassures us we do not need to be afraid, for the Lord is our HELPER. There is none that can harm us.

O – He is our OATH that keeps us from harm.

Ecclesiastes 8:2-5 stresses that when we have an oath with the King, his paths are ones of safety, no matter the winter winds that blow.

O – He is the OUTSTRETCHED arm that showers warmth on the earth.

Jeremiah 27:5 describes the creation of all things, for it is with God's OUTSTRETCHED arm that the earth and all its people were made. He gives the things he's created to anyone he pleases.

D – He brought life forth from the DUST of the earth.

Genesis 2:7 tells us the true power of God, for with the touch of his hand, he caused the DUST of the earth to become man.

I – He is the patron of ISRAEL, and he treats her as his beloved, showering love on his people.

Isaiah 44:6 names God as the king of ISRAEL. There is no other to which to turn for safety in the time of the storm, for as king, God has all authority and power.

E – He EXECUTES his will to do whatever he wishes.

Psalm 103:6 lets us know that in times of despair, we can fall into the Father's hands, for he EXECUTES his righteousness in all the land, giving justice to the oppressed.

In summary, when we bundle up in the Lord, we are safe against the rising storm.

Our JULY God

*Offering **Evangelism** to the World*

It's summer, the traditional time of family vacations, seaside picnics, and feasting with friends. It's a time for watermelons, barbecue, and cold iced tea.

When JULY comes around, we need to reach out and grab God's gift, for it's a time of warmth, leisure, and endless days in the sun.

It's JULY, the best month of the year.

Let's look at our JULY God:

J – He JOINS us together, that we may dine at his feast.

> There is no greater joy than to spend time among friends. 1 Corinthians 6:17 gives us the assurance that we are entwined with Christ in

the greatest friendship of all time.

U – The UTTERMOST parts of the earth are invited to his feast.

All are invited to the celebration of the Father. Acts 1:8 reveals that we shall draw his guests not only from our intimate circle of friends, but they shall come from the UTTERMOST parts of the world.

L – He LAYS out a barbecue spread of fabulous proportions.

When it is the time of feasting, we need have no fear of lack. Psalm 33:7 tells us that all God's bounty is stored away for us, and we cannot use it up.

Y – He holds our YESTERDAY securely in his hands.

When life is hard, and we fear God has forgotten us, all we have to do is look behind us. Hebrews 13:8 assures us we will find Jesus in our YESTERDAY, our today, and our tomorrow.

When we gather with God, and we invite our friends, we will enjoy a feast of the most bountiful kind. If we spread the news, soon our feast will encompass the whole world, and everyone will learn what God wants us to share.

His feast is ours, and everyone is invited to the table to dine with him.

In summary, when God lays out a spread, every attendee can dine to his heart's content.

Our LUSH God

*In **Worship** of Our Holy God*

When the days of spring linger, and the first buds have brought forth flowering bouquets, the world feels alive and new. All is green and LUSH, and anything seems possible.

We want these days to last forever. It's a time of relaxation and rejoicing. It's a time for thanksgiving to the God who created this world for us to enjoy.

Let's look at our LUSH God:

L – He is LIVING today, not dead as some might say.

> Many people point to the cross and claim that the promises of Jesus are hollow, for they cannot envision life coming out of death. Yes, Jesus did die on that rough tree. However, 1 Peter 2:4 tells us he is our LIVING Stone, rejected by man, but chosen by God.

Not only is Jesus still alive, he offers to bring us into spiritual life with him, giving us a place in the family of God.

U – He is UPRIGHT in all his ways, presenting unto us a perfect example.

As David wrote Psalm 25, he was at a pivotal point in his life. He was filled with distress as he pleaded with the Lord for intervention for Israel.

In Verse 8, he acknowledges the example God sets for humanity, telling us that the Lord is good and UPRIGHT, instructing man in the ways he should walk.

When God created man, he gave us our fallen natures. As a sign of his love, he continually holds his standard high, drawing our spirits to him.

S – He SUCCORS those who are in need of him, giving aid to the helpless.

Jesus didn't come to us as privileged royalty that could not understand our human condition. Instead, he became human so that he could know the depths of our trials. Hebrews 2:18 tells us that because he suffered and was tempted, he is able to provide SUCCOR to humanity. When we struggle to find our way to him, he holds out his hand in assistance.

Jesus comes to our aid when we reach out to him, for he has suffered as we suffer, and he has been tempted as we are tempted.

H – He is the HEALTH that restores us, returning green to our barren fields.

Israel had fallen low, and there was no good to be found in her future. Yet, in Jeremiah 30, we read of the prophesied return of Judah and Israel to the Promised Land.

In Verse 17, God tells Israel he will return HEALTH to her and heal her wounds. She has been an outcast, and he desires to make her strong once again.

When we face barren times, and all doors seem shut to us, God will restore us physically, mentally, and financially.

To summarize the message, when God's presence washes over our lives, he brings the lushness of new life. We are made new in him.

Our NIPPY God

*In **Worship** of Our Holy God*

It's on those sunny winter mornings when the world outside is crisp and clean that we feel drawn to the outdoors. We feel the brittle air slide down our throats, and the world seems brand new.

That's our God, bringing us the freshness of new life in the cold of winter. He is our NIPPY God, for there is nothing crisper and cleaner than God.

Let's look at our NIPPY God:

N – He comes as a great NOISE filled with heaven's glory.

> Ezekiel 43:2 reveals the coming of the majesty of God, for his voice makes the NOISE of many waters, and the earth shines with his glory.

I – He INHABITS that which he treasures.

Psalm 22:3 proclaims that God INHABITS the praises of his people. If we wish him to be near, we must lift our voices in celebration.

P – He provides a PARADISE for his children.

Luke 23:43 recounts Jesus speaking to the thief. "Today you will be with me in PARADISE." We will be with him in glory if only we believe on him.

P – He PRESERVES us in his safekeeping until that final day.

Job 7:20 calls God out as the one who PRESERVES all men. Even when our world crumbles around us, his hand keeps us from all harm.

Y – He is our YET God.

Nahum 2:8 shouts the magnificence of God. There is no great glory in living a life beaten down by sin. The glory comes to us in the word "yet." The Word says that even though the devil comes after us, when God speaks "yet," the enemy must flee.

In summary, Jesus daily brings us into a new life where we can be refreshed in our souls.

BIBLICAL

You Didn't Know Was in the Bible

The longest sentence in the New American Standard Bible contains 283 words!

(Check it out in Ephesians 1:3-14)

Our PICNIC God

*In **Worship** of Our Holy God*

A bright summer morning under a blue sky gives us the perfect opportunity to spend time in God's creation and reflect on him.

A PICNIC is the perfect time to do so. Our food is prepared ahead of time, there are no dishes to clean, and we can focus on his majesty. That's how God has provided for us. His salvation has been prepared ahead of time, he has cleansed our sins for us, and he wants nothing more than our praise.

Let's look at our PICNIC God:

P – He is the PEARL worth more than silver and gold.

Matthew 13:46 compares God to a PEARL that a man sells everything to obtain.

When we are willing to give up everything for

God, then we have learned his true value.

I – His IMAGE is reflected in us.

Genesis 1:26 tells us of God's decision to make man in his own IMAGE.

Our needs and desires reflect God's innate being. We are no mystery to him.

C – He CRIES unto us to come to him.

Micah 6:9 helps us understand how much God desires his creation to draw unto him, for he CRIES unto us. If we are wise, we will listen to the one who has all power under his command.

The voice of the Father is not far from us. Whether he chooses to speak to us from his Word or in a dream, he continually pulls us closer to him.

N – He is our NATHANAEL.

John 1:46-51 comprises Jesus' message of conversion in a nutshell. NATHANAEL begins with, "Can any good thing come out of Nazareth?" The passage ends with Nathanael's unmitigated belief in the Savior, and Jesus' words to him, "From now on, you will see the heavens open, and the angels of God descending before the Son of man."

When Jesus comes into our lives, his presence creates in us a new man.

I – He is our IMMORTAL savior, one who can never die.

1 Timothy 1:17 reveals the IMMORTAL nature of God, for he is the King eternal, invisible, the only wise God, due our honor and glory forever.

The lasting things of this world pale before the eternal nature of God. He watches the mountains crumble, becoming dust at his feet.

C – He is our unfailing CRUSE of oil.

In 1 Kings 17:14 Elijah told the widow that the CRUSE of oil would not fail until the day the Lord sent rain upon the earth.

When we face the dry days of summer, God is our everlasting source of sustenance.

To summarize the message, when we take time to reflect on the majesty of God, we will see that there is none other so wise and good, and he deserves our praise.

Our RECREATION God

In *Worship* of Our Holy God

In August, it's time to punch up the summer. It's a time of last hurrahs, one final week at the lake house, and one more cookout around a campfire. It's time to blow it up big, to make sure our summer extravaganza is one that no one will ever forget.

It's all about recreation; about doing things; about finding those activities we can't do any other time of the year. That's exactly what God is about. He loves to do things, to get involved in our lives in ways we can experience in no other fashion. He wants us to find our RECREATION in him.

Let's look at our RECREATION God:

R – He punches up our summer by granting our REQUESTS.

Philippians 4:6 tells us to prepare our summer

activity lists, because God is ready for the good times to begin.

E – He ESTABLISHES a party location for our big blowout.

Psalm 87:5 assures us that he will ESTABLISH a designated location for our campfire cookout, and everyone will wish to join in.

C – He COMES as our guest of honor.

1 Chronicles 16:33 tells us the celebration will begin when our Lord COMES to join in our summer extravaganza.

R – He parties all day long, even from the RISING of the sun.

Malachi 1:11 makes sure we understand that when we're jamming down on those hot summer days, we must praise the Lord, for the RISING sun has brought the presence of God to dwell among us.

E – He brings EACH of us a special reason to enjoy the summer sun.

Acts 2:3 envisions EACH of Jesus' followers bathed with the fire of the Holy Spirit. None were excluded, and all joined in the festivities.

A – He ALLOWS us to have fun at our summer bash.

Romans 14:22 encourages us to be happy in doing that which God ALLOWS us to do. What is right and good for us is between us and our God and should not be held up in judgment against others.

T – He is our TRUSTED party planner, and there is no good thing that he leaves out.

Ephesians 1:13 is our convincing example of God as the horn of plenty, for the Word says that God is the one in whom we have TRUSTED; the word of truth; the gospel of our salvation; and he seals us with the spirit of promise.

I – He is the IMAGE of our good time and our example to follow.

Genesis 1:27 tells us God shaped us in his IMAGE, and when he declares the party is on, we should be ready to rock.

O – He ORDAINS that our party will be a success, and that all who show up will have a grand time.

Isaiah 26:12 specifies that our celebration in him

is a direct result of God choosing to elevate our gathering from a simple dinner to a game-filled festival centered on him. He ORDAINS our fun.

N – He is the good NEWS that our cold sodas and iced teas are being served on the patio.

Proverbs 25:25 compares our Lord to good NEWS from a distant land. Hearing of his approach is better than a cold drink on a hot day.

God wants us to be doing things all the time, whether winning souls for the kingdom, having a celebration in his honor, or simply being a committed child of the King. We see how he wants us to be by his example. We find his example in his written Word.

In summary, when we become like Jesus, we will find joy and fun in our walk with him.

Our RIPE God

In Pursuit of the **Kingdom of God**

America is a now culture. We find it difficult to plant a seed and wait for it to grow. Instant coffee; microwaves; drive-thru meals. We want it now.

However, some things need to fully mature. Cut a green cantaloupe, and it's tasteless. Pluck a strawberry too early, and we will spit it out. An unripe banana finds difficulty going down.

When we let God have his way in our lives, and we are patient with his guidance, we will know the sweetness of our RIPE God.

Let's look at our RIPE God:

R – He requires our labor, for the harvest is RIPE.

> Joel 3:13 tells us the season is upon us. We are to labor for God, not the other way round. He is our master, and we are his servants.

I – He goes with us and gives us INCREASE.

> Zechariah 10:8 tells us that not only will God bless his children, he will also bless those we come into contact with. The fullness of his IN-CREASE will overflow our storehouses, and others will know that God is with us.

P – He desires that we PROSPER in all that we do.

> 3 John 2 tells us that when our soul prospers, God will also PROSPER us in health and material wealth. Our first step is to draw close to the Lord, so that he can bless us in other ways.

E – He is the EVIDENCE of things not seen.

> Hebrews 11:1 tells us that in our faith we find the EVIDENCE of our invisible God. It's when we fully trust in him that he becomes real in our life.

To summarize the message, we will know the majesty of God only when we become fully mature in him.

Our SEA God

*In Pursuit of the **Kingdom of God***

As vast as the continents on our world are, they pale in comparison to the SEA. The oceans of this world stretch for three times the distance of the land, and they plunge deeper than the highest mountains we can climb. The resources of the sea are so fantastic as to seem without end.

That's just like our God. He reaches far and above anything we can know, and his bounty is without end. There is no greater resource than the Father in heaven.

Let's look at our SEA God:

S – His STOREHOUSES are laid up for us, that we might have access to all the good things in his creation.

Psalm 33:7 tells us that "He gathereth the

waters of the sea together as an heap: he layeth up the depth in STOREHOUSES."

All the things on this earth are his, and as deep as the oceans are is how much he accumulates for our benefit.

E – He ENRICHES all the world with the sea's bounty.

Psalm 65:9 describes how God spreads his blessings over the whole of the earth. "Thou visitest the earth, and waterest it: thou greatly ENRICHEST it with the river of God, which is full of water: thou preparest them corn, when thou hast so provided for it."

Without the oceans of this world, there would be little rainfall on the dry land. It's through the salt nuclei from the ocean spray and evaporation of surface water that the nourishing rains bring life to the dry continents.

A – He ANOINTS us with the joy of his creation, that we might find fulfillment in him.

Psalm 45:7 assures us that God rewards us for our dedication to him. This verse tells us that "Thou lovest righteousness, and hatest wickedness: therefore God, thy God, hath ANOINTED thee with the oil of gladness above thy fellows."

All of the world's abundance is God's, and he does with it as he will. What is his will? He wishes those that love the right and hate the wrong to be glad in him. There can be no greater gift than that.

When we follow after the God of all creation, we need have no fear that we will run out of his good things. After all, he created them all, and he who created everything can never run short of what resides in the palm of his hand.

In summary, God's blessings fill the entire earth, and there is no end to what he can do for us.

Our SPICE God

*In Pursuit of the **Kingdom of God***

October brings the first true chills of the fall season. The winds turn to the north, and the changing leaves rattle in the breeze. We rub our arms, and we head for the fire. That's where we will be warm.

There's another way to warm ourselves, also. We can down a deep draught of SPICE tea, that flavorful brew that fills us with an intoxicating plethora of scents and tastes.

That's how our God comes to us. When the winds of life turn against us, and we search for answers to warm us, God fills us with the scents of his SPICES, and he warms us as he goes down.

Let's look at our SPICE God and see how he renews us each day:

S – He SHINES his face on us.

Numbers 6:25 falls in the middle of a priestly blessing spoken on behalf of the Israelites. It tells us "the Lord [will] make his face to SHINE upon you and be gracious to you."

When our days appear darkened by clouds and cold winds, the glorious face of God is just on the other side of the clouds. He is still there and waiting on us to find him.

P – He offers us PARADISE at his side.

Luke 23:43 reveals an intimate moment as Jesus hangs on the cross. He speaks to the criminal suspended at his side. "Truly, I say to you, today you will be with me in PARADISE."

Talk about brushing the chill away! What better words can we hear to spice up our day?

I – He molds us into his IMAGE, making us like him.

1 Corinthians 15:49 concludes Paul's exhortation concerning the resurrection of our earthly bodies. He tells us that "just as we have borne the image of the man of dust, we shall also bear the IMAGE of the man of heaven."

Certainly we are human, but that is a temporary state. We will take on the likeness of God, and every chill wind will be left behind.

C – He speaks CHEER into our dreary days.

Matthew 14:27 gives us a glimpse of how attuned Jesus is to our human nature. As he walked across the waters of the sea, he called to his frightened disciples, "Take heart; it is I. Do not be afraid."

The King James Version says, "Be of good CHEER." When we intentionally brighten our outlook, we will find the world around us brightens, also.

E – He ESTEEMS us highly because of our labors.

1 Thessalonians 5:13 speaks to our endeavors for Christ. Paul encourages our fellow believers "to ESTEEM [us] very highly in love because of [our] work."

When we feel the first chilly drafts of fall, we need to increase our labors for the Lord. Others will heap praise and thankfulness on us, and their words will be as the warmth of God's everlasting love.

As ordinary people, born into humanity and living upon this earth, we need to feel the encompassing touch of God's love. He offers it to us freely, adding the SPICE of his blessings as he reaches out unto us.

In summary, when we need encouragement, God will be there, and he will lift us up above our problems.

BIBLICAL *Trivia*

You Didn't Know Was in the Bible

The shortest complete chapter in the Bible has fewer words than the Lord's Prayer.

(Check it out in Psalm 117)

Our TENDER God

*Finding **Faith** in the Word of Christ*

Spring is a time of new life. The lamb walks at its mother's side. Baby birds sing in their nests. Leaves shimmer with the bright green of first growth.

These things speak to our hearts, because they need TENDER care. The lamb will falter without the shepherd's touch. Baby birds cannot feed themselves. First foliage can be crushed by the brush of a careless touch.

Our God knows our fragile moments, and he is TENDER towards us. When we step out on his word, and we find it difficult to trust in him, he offers us his special care. His TENDER touch can be felt in the brush of his hand, and as he holds us gently in his arms.

The Psalms give us repeated assurances of God's TENDER nature.

Let's take a look at our TENDER God:

T – He is the TENDER breath of refreshing when our lives seem to close in on us.

Psalm 103:4 tells us that life is destruction. Yet, we are redeemed, for our great King will crown us with his lovingkindness, and he will shower us with his eternal mercies.

Our God spreads the flowers upon the hillside, bringing new life to the barren fields. He will do the same for us.

E – He EXALTS us above the misery of our circumstances.

Psalm 89:19 gives us the example of David, telling us how God provides help to his chosen ones. When God comes on the scene, he EXALTS us from out of the crowd, and we will stand tall in him.

We are not ordinary in the sight of God. We are extraordinary, and he wants us to be a beacon for him.

N – He knows the NUMBERS of all that is, all that was, and all that will ever be. Nothing escapes his supernatural knowledge.

Psalm 147:4 describes God's mighty power. He knows the NUMBERS of the stars, calling each one by name.

When our Father cares enough about his creation to name each and every star, how can he not care for our wellbeing?

D – He is our secure DWELLING, our place of rest in the time of the storm.

Psalm 4:8 offers us rest in him. We can sleep in the peace of the Lord, for in him, we DWELL in safety.

God is better than locks on our windows and firewalls on our computers. He protects our hearts from the sin that besets us.

E – He guards us on EVERY side, so that nothing can come against us.

Psalm 71:21 reassures us that when trouble comes our way, God will give us increase, and when others battle against us, God will be our comfort on EVERY side.

This world will bring us challenges, but we can find our comfort in our Christian fellowship and in the knowledge that our salvation is secure in Christ.

R – He is a RIVER that waters our soul with his hand of provisions and pleasure.

Psalm 36:8 reveals the mighty resources of our God, for a RIVER of joy flows from him, and in his house, we will find our satisfaction.

We need no other source than our God, for when the world falls short is exactly when he steps in to give his joy to us in excess.

In summary, we can trust in our God, for his heart is filled with tenderness toward us.

Our TRIP God

*Finding **Faith** in the Word of Christ*

For those of us with children, sometimes summer seems to stretch into eternity. If traveling to summer camps and ferrying carloads of kiddos to VBS aren't enough, how can we stand to drip dry another pint-sized swimsuit? We want to pull out our hair with the absurdity of it all. Aren't there any other adults out there in the world to talk to at all?

When we reach our limit, it's time to plan a TRIP. We need to change our surroundings, step off the merry-go-round, and find our milk chocolate wonderland. It's that break with routine that will help us survive until we can pack the little ones back off to school once again.

God is that break in our routine. He is our TRIP to our milk chocolate wonderland. He will be the one that helps us to survive the summer until we can take a deep breath and relax once again.

Let's take a look into the wonders of our TRIP God:

T – He welcomes the TRAVELER into his embrace.

> Job is an archetype of the Christ, for he presents to us the good and perfect man brought to death and returned to the bounty of life. In Job 31:32 we read that no TRAVELER passed Job's door that he was not invited to stay the night.

R – He honors our every REQUEST that our travels be successful.

> Our Christian walk is a trip through the minefields of a sinful world. Philippians 4:6 reassures us that as we travel, we do not need to be anxious. Through prayer and supplication, we can make our REQUESTS known unto God. We can travel in the safety of his assurances.

I – He INSTRUCTS us in order to guide us on our way.

> Acts 18:24-28 tells the story of Apollos. He traveled, fervently preaching the gospel, even though he only knew a portion of God's mystery revealed through Christ. Priscilla and Aquila INSTRUCTED him more thoroughly so that his footsteps would lead others closer to the cross.

P – He PREVAILS over the whole earth, no matter where we may travel.

> Noah, whether by man's intent or God's design, was one of the most traveled men on earth. He journeyed on the ark across the stormy seas for 150 days. In Genesis 7:19, 24 we read that there was nowhere God's flood did not reach out to hold his ship afloat. No matter how far Noah voyaged, God's hand PREVAILED over all creation.

Do we want to take a trip? Ask for God's blessing first, and he will be at our side the entire way, and no evil thing can come against us.

In summary, when we travel with God, not even the best travel service in the world can surpass the protecting hand of our almighty Father.

Our VIBRANT God

In **Worship** of Our Holy God

Take the crocus. It's the simplest of flowers, yet it does something no other flower does. It blooms through the final blanket of the early spring snowfall, sticking its tentative shoot upward, even as the rest of the world hunkers in redoubt against the bitter winds.

The crocus doesn't see the icy covering over its head as a reason to give up on life. Rather, it becomes a challenge. The crocus knows it's time to bloom, and it does so in spite of the challenges, forming a VIBRANT carpet of color against the stark landscape of retreating winter.

God encourages us to do the same, for we abide in his sustenance, and it is with his authority that we break through that which entombs us, reaching our arms into the sun, and finding that which is waiting on us: the VIBRANT brilliance of God's presence on our faces, warming us with his glory, and inviting us to rejoice in him.

Let's take a look at our VIBRANT God:

V – He is the VICTORY that comes after the struggle.

> 1 Chronicles 29:11 describes the magnificence of our holy Lord, for his is the greatness, the power, the glory, and the VICTORY; for there is nothing in the heavens that does not belong to him.
>
> Even in something as insignificant as a flower struggling against the chill of early spring, God trumpets his success in the blooms that carpet the land.

I – He is our INHERITANCE, the proof of his faith in us.

> Ephesians 1:11 leaves no room for doubt, for in this passage, we can find the assurance that if we allow God to perform his will in us, he will reward us with the beauty that we call heaven.
>
> The flower under the soil, encased in its protective bulb, cannot see the sun, nor can it embrace the sky. Yet the sun and the sky are there anyway. Even so, the crocus reaches through the chill soil, and breaking the snow's crust, finds

that which is its promise: sun, refreshing, and life. Its INHERITANCE is already there; it only has to reach for it.

B – He BRINGS us his hand of blessing, giving us fresh life for our sustenance.

Psalm 1:3 is a richly encouraging passage, for we learn that if we sink our roots into the waters of life, God's power will BRING forth fruit in the coming season, our leaves will not wither, and we will prosper in all that we do.

Our God turns the earth on its axis, and he carpets our world with the sun's warmth. It is his gracious love that BRINGS life to his children. The snow is for a season, and when we reach toward him, we will find his blessings.

R – He REMEMBERS us, even when the world buries us in pain.

Genesis 9:15 is the culmination of one of the most horrific stories in the Bible. Man has been so evil that God has destroyed them all, except for one man's family, Noah's. Yet, even in all the destruction, God REMEMBERS his covenant with Noah and all living creatures, and he vows never again to destroy his creation with a flood.

When we feel we can't find the light of day, God has not forgotten us. We can reach up through the bitterest circumstance, and the warmth of God's presence will remind us that he REMEMBERS us.

A – He is ALTOGETHER everything we need.

Psalm 19:9 exposes the core of our relationship with God. There is nothing we need, other than him. Our respect for the Lord purifies us. His judgments are dependable and trustworthy.

What we must remember is that God does not cover us with lifelessness. Rather, he gives us new life. All we have to do is listen to him, and when he says grow, we stretch and grow, right through the crust of the snow. Remember, he is ALTOGETHER everything we need.

N – His NAME is that rock upon which we can stand.

Isaiah 50:10 gives us no room for misunderstanding. When the circumstances of life keep the warmth of God's love from us, all we have to do is trust in the NAME of the Lord, and we will know the brilliance of his power and might in our lives.

The power of God will be the source of our

strength, just as the sun causes the flower to grow. All we need to do is believe on his NAME.

T – He is the TREASURE that we seek.

Deuteronomy 28:12 reveals our God's TREASURE house, for his good gifts are in the rain that falls upon the land, in the crops we harvest, and in the great riches we amass.

When God chooses to bless us, the unexpected spring snows that remind us of the desolate winter season must melt before him. We will be free to reach toward life and prosperity, for all the TREASURE of God's storehouses is ours to enjoy.

In summary, God's presence is VIBRANT in our lives, for he is our INHERITANCE, our SUSTENANCE, and our great TREASURE.

Our WINDY God

*In **Worship** of Our Holy God*

The snowmen have melted and the ice is gone from the roof. Strings of lights are put away for another holiday season, and the chocolates of Valentine's Day are long since eaten.

The season is changing once again, and we can look forward to the bright days of spring.

However, we cannot second guess the weather. All it takes is a blast of artic air, and it is winter all over again.

That is our WINDY God, reminding us of his power and might, even as we begin to relax our guard. He is in the wind, and he goes and does as he will.

Let's look at our WINDY God:

W – He fills the WHOLE earth with his magnificent

presence.

Daniel 2:35 describes the awesome power of the Lord, for in Nebuchadnezzar's dream, a rock first crushed the kingdom, then the rock grew to encompass the WHOLE earth. That rock was God.

When the devil comes at us, and we see his presence as overwhelming, we must remember that our God is as big as the world, and he can crush the enemy with the smallest of movements.

I – He is our INHERITANCE as blood-washed Christians.

Colossians 1:12 tells us to give our thanks unto the Father. It is by the hand of our God Almighty that we receive the bountiful blessing of our expected glory to come.

Our situation on this world is not God's final plan for us. Whether we are blessed with material goods or simply eking out a living, our true wealth will come in heaven. We are spiritual beings, and what we can touch now is only temporary. Heaven is our INHERITANCE as children of the Light.

N – He is our NOURISHER and our giver of good

gifts.

> Ruth 4:15 illustrates how God cares for those who follow after him. This verse sings with praises to God, for he is Naomi's restorer and the NOURISHER of her old age.

> When we see the future as bleak, and despair fills our days, we can look upward, for we have a God who sees our every need. He will come to us, and he will provide that which we didn't know we needed.

D – He is the DIVINE that keeps his promises unto everlasting.

> 2 Peter 1:4 gives us the assurances that God cannot be other than God. It is in his nature to be DIVINE, for he has the power to give life unto all creation.

> When we worry that our season of harsh weather will never end, we must remember that God is by his very nature the giver of life. He will come unto us once again, gifting unto us his glory and blessings.

Y – He is our YEA and amen God.

> Psalm 68:3 encourages us to rejoice in the

presence of the Lord, for if we are righteous, we can be glad in our Creator. We are to lift our hands in praise and sing unto him.

We do not rejoice in our circumstances. Rather, we rejoice in the one who made all creation, for he is the one in whom we can say: YEA, let them exceedingly rejoice, for he is the king of all the earth.

In summary, when we take time to be reminded of the greatness of our God, he won't have to do it for us.

Our YAM God

*Finding **Faith** in the Word of Christ*

A yam is not a sweet potato. The yam is a black-skinned root vegetable with bark-like skin, native to Africa and Asia. In parts of the United States, we use the words interchangeably, but they are not one and the same.

The same is true of our God. Many people confuse him with money, happiness, or a season of the year. However, he is none of those things.

Like our God, the yam is a staple source of food, one whose name actually means "to eat." Like the yam, our God is our source of sustenance, and without him we cannot live.

Let's look at our YAM God:

Y – He brings us the vigor of YOUTH once again.

    Psalm 103:5 proclaims the goodness of our

eternal God, for he will satisfy us with good things, so that our YOUTH is renewed like that of the eagle on wing.

A – He APPEARS to us in all his magnificence.

Numbers 20:6 reveals what God wishes from us. Moses and Aaron fell to their faces before God, and the glory of the Lord APPEARED unto them.

M – He MEASURES out to us more than our cup can hold.

Ephesians 4:7 encourages us to be prepared for the glory of Jesus's grace, for it will be MEASURED out to us according to the gifts of Christ.

What can we learn from this? The things of this world are good, as are the sweet potatoes we consume at mealtime. However, it is our YAM God that provides the sustenance that enables us to survive and prosper in our faith.

To summarize the message, when we dine on God, we become fat with his goodness and grace.

Coming to Christ
In Three Easy Steps

If you do not know Christ as your personal savior, there is no better time than the present to turn your life over to him.

- Step 1 is to admit that you are human, God is God, and you need his grace.
- Step 2 is to place your belief in him. You must accept that he is the Son of the Eternal God, and through his death on the cross, he can give you new life.
- Step 3 is to turn from your previous ways and receive the hope of Jesus' power in you.

Fill in the following information as a testament to your decision to accept Jesus as your Savior.

I, _____, accept Jesus
                print your full name

as my personal savior on _____.
                                  today's date

_____
              your signature

Look for these additional topics on the MyChurchNotes.net website:

2 Timothy
Beatitudes
Discipleship
Evangelism
Faith
Family
Healing
Hope
Kingdom of God
Money
Prayer
Relationships
Repentance
Salvation
Worship

MyChurchNotes.net is a faith-based ministry founded on a belief in the Father, the Son, and the Holy Spirit. All MyChurchNotes.net articles are based on Scripture and created especially for MyChurchNotes.net.

Our Mission Statement is to take the Word of God into all the nations, and proclaim that he is Lord!

If you enjoyed
Finding God Through Acronyms,
please visit us at our website:

www.MyChurchNotes.net

We look forward to hearing from you.

Website and Publication Powered by:

Bright Herd . . . for All Your Website and
Media Design Needs.
www.brightherd.com
contact@brightherd.com

www.ingramcontent.com/pod-product-compliance
Lightning Source LLC
Chambersburg PA
CBHW061445040426
42450CB00007B/1226